The Disgusting

make your own
Fake
Vomit

Julia Garstecki

BLACK
RABBIT
BOOKS

Hi Jinx is published by Black Rabbit Books
P.O. Box 3263, Mankato, Minnesota, 56002.
www.blackrabbitbooks.com
Copyright © 2019 Black Rabbit Books

Marysa Storm, editor; Michael Sellner, designer;
Omay Ayres, photo researcher

Library of Congress Cataloging-in-Publication Data
Names: Garstecki, Julia, author.
Title: Make your own fake vomit / by Julia Garstecki.
Description: Mankato, Minnesota : Black Rabbit Books, [2019]
Series: Hi jinx. The disgusting crafter | Includes bibliographical
references and index. | Audience: Ages 9-12.
Audience: Grades 4-6.
Identifiers: LCCN 2017055769 (print) |
LCCN 2017056340 (ebook) |
ISBN 9781680726329 (e-book) |
ISBN 9781680726268 (library binding) |
ISBN 9781680727623 (paperback)
Subjects: LCSH: Food–Juvenile humor.
Practical jokes–Juvenile literature.
Vomiting–Juvenile humor.
Classification: LCC TX355 (ebook)
LCC TX355 .G365 2019 (print)
DDC 745.5–dc23
LC record available at
https://lccn.loc.gov/2017055769

Printed in the United States. 5/18

Image Credits

Shutterstock: Alex Tihonovs, Back Cover (bkgd); anfisa
focusova, 3 (bkgd); Arcady, 3 (note); binik, Cover (splatter
bkgd), 6–7 (splatter bkgd), 14–15 (splatter bkgd); blambca,
1 (vomit), 19 (vomit), 20 (vomit); Elizabeth A.Cummings, 7
(food coloring), 10 (food coloring), 15 (food coloring), 17 (food
coloring); Jamesbin, 14 (pot, spoon), 22 (pot, spoon); John T Takai, 7
(bags, microwave), 8 (bags, microwave), 15 (bag, crackers), 16 (bags,
crackers), 17 (bag); Katerina Davidenko, 18–19 (hill); K.Sorokin, 11
(clock); lineartestpilot, 7 (fork), 8 (fork); mohinimurti, 7 (bkgd),
15 (bkgd); opicobello, 12–13; owatta, 7 (wax paper);
Pasko Maksim, Back Cover (top), 11 (top), 23, 24;
Pitju, 21 (page curl); Ron Dale, 5 (top), 6 (top),
20 (top); Ron Leishman, Cover (people, goo), 1,
2–3, 4, 5 (girl, vomit), 6 (people, stove, vomit), 7
(bowl, baking dish), 8 (bowls), 10 (bowl, baking
dish), 10–11, 12, 13, 14 (dog, girl), 15 (rolling pin),
16 (rolling pin), 17 (hands, vomit), 18, 19 (boy,
tree), 20 (birds, vomit), 21 (cow), 22 (girl, dog); Sofia
Shimanovskaia, Cover (splatter), 6–7 (splatter), 11–15
(splatter); totallyplc, 8 (arrows), 10 (arrow), 11 (arrow);
Yusak_P, 7 (cups), 8 (cups), 15 (spoons), 16 (spoon) Every
effort has been made to contact copyright holders for material
reproduced in this book. Any omissions will be rectified in
subsequent printings if notice is given to the publisher.

contents

Did you know crafting in the kitchen is actually science? It's true. Making mixtures is something scientists do all the time. So grab your lab coat (or an apron). It's time to mix and measure your way to some fake vomit.

Chapter 1
Be a Disgusting Crafter

Throwing up for real is never fun. But fake puke can be a blast! You can use it to fool your friends or prank your parents. There are many ways to make vomit. Like the real thing, it makes a difference what you put into it!

Chapter 2
Let's Make!

This recipe makes solid puke that's easy to move. Lay it on the kitchen floor to gross out unsuspecting family members.

What You'll Need

1/3 cup (79 milliliters) water

1/3 cup (79 ml) mashed fruit or vegetables (Blueberries, bananas, and peas work well.)

2 .25-ounce (7-gram) packets of **gelatin**

microwave

wax paper

large baking dish

liquid food coloring (optional)

fork

microwave-safe bowl

Directions

 Pour the water into the bowl.

 Microwave the water for 1 minute or until it's boiling.

 Add the gelatin to the water.

 Stir the gelatin with the fork. The gelatin should **dissolve**.

 The mixture can get clumpy. Squish the lumps with the back of the fork.

 Mix the mashed fruit into the gelatin and water.

6. Add a few drops of food coloring to the mixture, if you'd like. Orange or red-pink are good vomit colors.

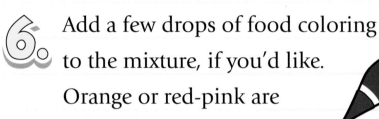

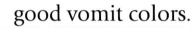

7. Place a sheet of wax paper on the bottom of the baking dish.

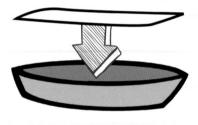

8. Pour the mixture onto the wax paper.

9. Let the mixture cool. This will take about 30 minutes.

10. Peel your creation off the wax paper. It's ready to use!

11

Using Your Vomit

This vomit works best on a flat surface. All you have to do is place the puke. Then wait until you hear a grossed-out family member **shrieking**.

You can also make **gagging** noises to go with it. Wait until a family member checks on you. Then show off your masterpiece.

Feelin' Crummy?

This recipe is super simple. Just a handful of crackers can make a great pile of puke. It won't harden right away either. It's great for times when you need a soupier puke.

What You'll Need

plastic storage baggie (sandwich-sized or larger)

rolling pin

small handful of crackers (Saltine crackers work well.)

5 to 6 tablespoons (74 to 89 ml) water

liquid food coloring (optional)

Directions

1. Place the crackers in the bag, and seal the bag.

2. Use the rolling pin to break the crackers into small pieces.

3. Place 1 tablespoon of water in the baggie.

4. Reseal the bag, and squish the crackers with your hands.

 5. Add more water until the mix looks like puke. Add only about a tablespoon of water at a time.

 6. Add a few drops of food coloring to the cracker mixture, if you want. A lovely green might be nice. Seal the bag and squish the mixture to mix in the color.

Using Your Vomit

You can leave this vomit for people to find. Just be careful where you put it. Like real vomit, it can be a pain to clean up! Don't want to just leave puke for people to find? In that case, add a few more tablespoons of water to the mixture. Then use it to puke right before your target's eyes.

Chapter 3

Get in on the Hi Jinx

Throwing up is disgusting. But it's important for the body to do. Food poisoning is one reason you might throw up. The stomach flu is another.

Humans aren't the only creatures with reasons to puke. Snakes might throw up meals that are too big. Some birds even vomit as self-defense. Real puke has many uses. How many can you think up for the fake stuff?

Take It One Step More

1. Look around your kitchen. What else can you add to your puke?

2. Can you think of any times puke pranks might not be **appropriate**?

3. Animals throw up for many reasons. Research more reasons animals puke.

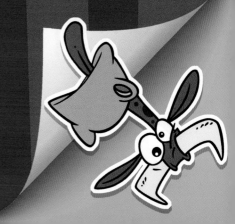

GLOSSARY

appropriate (up-PROH-pree-it)—right or suited for some purpose or situation

dissolve (di-ZOLV)—to mix with a liquid and become part of the liquid

gag (GAG)—to vomit or feel like vomiting

gelatin (JEL-uh-tn)—a gummy or sticky protein made by boiling animal tissues and used especially as food

shriek (SHREEK)—a loud high-pitched cry or sound

BOOKS

Crispin, Sam. *Vomit! Your Body at Its Grossest!*
New York: Gareth Stevens Publishing, 2018.

Huffman, Julie. *101 Ways to Gross Out Your Friends.*
Lake Forest, CA: Quarto Publishing Group USA
Inc., 2016.

Lowell, Barbara. *Bodily Functions.* The Amazing
Human Body. Mankato, MN: Black Rabbit
Books, 2019.

WEBSITES

How to Make Fake Vomit
www.youtube.com/watch?v=U_xtZQtpusw

What's Puke?
kidshealth.org/en/kids/puke.html

You May Be Eating Vomit, and More Bizarre
Barf Facts
**news.nationalgeographic.com/2017/03/vomit-
throw-up-snakes-pythons-vultures/**

TIPS AND TRICKS

Adults can be helpful. Don't be afraid to ask for help with any part of your disgusting craft.

Don't like how the first recipe smells? Add some vanilla extract. It should improve the scent.

To store the first recipe, place it in a large plastic storage baggie. Keep it in a cool place.

To cool the first recipe faster, put it in the refrigerator.